AND WE RISE

AND WE RISE

THE CIVIL RIGHTS MOVEMENT IN POEMS

Erica Martin

VIKING

VIKING
An imprint of Penguin Random House LLC, New York

First published in the United States of America by Philomel Books,
an imprint of Penguin Random House LLC, 2022

Text copyright © 2022 by Halcyenda Erica Martin

Text of "Letter from a Birmingham Jail" courtesy of public domain

Image credits on page 135

Visit us online at penguinrandomhouse.com.

Library of Congress Cataloging-in-Publication Data is available.

Printed in the United States of America

ISBN 9780593352526

2nd Printing

Edited by Liza Kaplan

Design by Monique Sterling

Text set in Freight

for you, Ma, for marching for me

It's 1877 when
Jim Crow laws say it's
        acceptable
        legal
        lawful
to segregate Blacks
&
        whites
based on the color of
their skin.

In

        schools

        hospitals

        churches

        cemeteries

        prisons

        public transit

        restaurants—

if you were not
          white
you were lesser
          less than
human.

For years
&
years
&
years
&
years

nothing changed,

until 1954
when the Supreme Court reversed its decision
     & ruled segregation unconstitutional.

Yet still,
nothing changed.

Because a ruling is only as effective
as its real-world execution.

the Supreme Court rules

in 1896
Blacks are
"Separate but Equal"

yet
outside
in the middle of July
in Birmingham, Alabama,
sweat drips

d
o
w
n

your forehcad
your neck
your back

drenching

your shirt
your shorts
your socks

                                      s e p a r a t e
                                      but equal

you find a water fountain
your water fountain
and press the small rusty button

water arches
                        up

                                    and out
waiting
            for your
puck ered
            lips

                                      s e p a r a t e
                                      but equal

only

it's hot
brown
tastes like dirt

you glance around
checking for *them*

then

sneak a sip
from *their* fountain

                                        s e p a r a t e
                                        but equal

it's cold
ice-cold
and refreshing

you sigh

s e p a r a t e

but equal
you are
not.

PART ONE

ONE STEP FORWARD, TWO STEPS BACK

the Civil Rights Movement

was more than just
Dr. King
      marching,
Rosa Parks
      sitting,
Malcolm X
      fighting.

it was

your mom
your grandma
your best friend's great-aunt.

it was
everyday people

like you   and me.

Brown v. Board of Education

+

inherently unequal, an unconstitutional violation of the fourteenth amendment

=

white schools

+

███ schools

=

a great day for America and its court.

= segregation in public schools   now illegal

in theory.

separate but equal

w a s   perfectly fine

you're only a *nigger*

if you step out of

                    line

A group of teenage boys protesting school integration in Montgomery, Alabama, 1963.

SIGNS, EVERYWHERE YOU GO . . . whites only whites only whites only whites only whites only whites only whites only whites only whites only whites only whites only whites only whites only whites only whites only whites only whites only whites only w¹ ⁻nly whites only whites only whites only whites only whites only whites ⁻⁻es only whites only whites only whites only whites on⁻ whites only whites only whites only whites ⁻hites only whites only whites only whites ⁻ whites only whites only whites only white whites only whites only whites only wh⁻ whites only whites only whites only whites only v whites only whites only whites only whites only whites onl⁻ whites only whites only whites only whites only whites o⁻ whites only whites only whites only whites only whites whites only whites only whites only whites only whites only whit whites only whites only whites only whites only whites only whites onÿ whites only whites only whites only whites only whites only whites only whites only whites only whites ⁻ whites only whites only whites only whites only whites only .ites only whites only whites only whites only whites only whm. whites only whites only whites only whites only whites only .y whites only whites only whites only whites only whites only whites only .nly whites only
WHITES ONLY
whites only

for colored

        their (other) signs read

funny thing is

white is still a color

1955

MARCH 2

I.

BEFORE ROSA PARKS
before the Montgomery boycott sparked—

Claudette Colvin
was riding home
with schoolmates
in the whites-only zone

on a full bus
headed across town
a white woman showed up
and wanted to sit down

get up the driver said
Claudette did not
three students moved
as she maintained her spot

I paid my fare,
it's my constitutional right!
she wasn't giving in
without a fight

get up, get up
a command on repeat
still Claudette remained
firmly in her seat

two police officers boarded
and gave her another chance
Claudette refused
and held tight to her stance

they grabbed her by the wrists
and dragged her out the door
the books in her lap
falling to the floor

nigger bitch they teased
as they drove to the city jail
she wasn't allowed a phone call
led her straight to a cell

three bare walls
a toilet and a cot
they locked her in
and left her to rot

she fell to her knees
and began to cry
praying, asking
why, God, why?

bailed out by her pastor
she was finally free
to pursue justice
and equal liberty

via the courts
she would sue
with three other plaintiffs
their litigation overdue

Browder v. Gayle
won their heated case
buses could not be segregated
by something as trivial as race

Claudette Colvin
fifteen years old
her story in studies
largely untold

II.

when you're raised by your   great-aunt
                                        &
                 your   great-uncle,

what else are you to become
but a girl destined
for greatness?

A POLIO SURVIVOR

with a s-s-stutter

    and a suitcase full of jokes

        he laughed all the way to Mississippi,

Emmett Till lying in bed, smiling, January 1, 1954.

        America's favorite punchline.

1955

AUGUST 28

I.

THIS IS THE STORY OF EMMETT TILL

about the way he was ultimately killed

he crossed his murderers at
Bryant's Grocery and Meat Market
no one would save him
no one would stop it

dumped in the river
after taking a bullet to the head
all because of something
a frightened white woman said

the echo of a whistle
the ghost of a lie
told by Carolyn Bryant
so that nigger had to die

kidnapped from his house
in the middle of the night
well, that's what he gets
for not being white!

stupid nigger
time to learn his place
the Black man is the inferior
of the human race

beat in a barn
until barely alive
then it was decided
he needn't survive

into the Tallahatchie
his body was tossed
just another nigger
not really a loss

a fourteen-year-old boy
resigned to this fate
America cared about Emmett
just a little too late

II.

his whistle lives on
in the Mississippi breeze

rattling windows
of that crumbling grocery   store

SUMMER
1955

days
weeks
months pass

and still

every day
you step into that hot metal bus
and head to the back

the very back

where it smells of piss and sweat.

People always say that I didn't give up my seat because I was tired, but that isn't true. I was not tired physically, or no more tired than I usually was at the end of a working day. I was not old, although some people have an image of me as being old then. I was forty-two. No, the only tired I was, was tired of giving in.

—Rosa Parks

1955
DECEMBER 1

tired is when

the souls of the enslaved
who jumped ship to sea
hold you down
won't let you be

anchor your feet
to the Atlantic floor
hands around your ankles
their message: *no more*

Rosa Parks's mug shot, 1955.

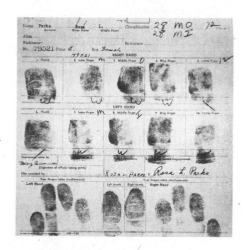

Rosa Parks's fingerprint card, 1955.

1955

DECEMBER 5

OUT OF JAIL

to walk

the streets
of Montgomery, Alabama,

     to boycott the buses
          for as long as it takes

walk

to school
to church
to work

walk

for miles and miles
feet blistering and sore

walk

when your breath clouds the air

when the sun burns your skin

ignore the pain

just
        walk

as the days pass
as the seasons shift
as the year turns over
and nothing
changes
for

1

2

3

4

5

6

7

8

9

10

11

12

13

14

15

16

17

18

19

20

21

22

23

24

25

26

27

28

29

30

31

32

33

34

35

36

37

38

39

40

41

42

43

44

45

46

47

48

49

50

51

52

53

54

55

56

57

58

59

60

61

62

63

64

65

66

67

68

69

70

71

72

73

74

75

76

77

78

79

80

81

82

83

84

85

86

87

88

89

90

91

92

93

94

95

96

97

98

99

100

101

102

103

104

105

106

107

108

109

110

111

112

113

114

115

116

117

118

119

120

121

122

123

124

125

126

127

128

129

130

131

132

133

134

135

136

137

138

139

140

141

142

143

144

145

146

147

148

149

150

151

152

153

154

155

156

157

158

159

160

161

162

163

164

165

166

167

168

169

170

171

172

173

174

175

176

177

178

179

180

181

182

183

184

185

186

187

188

189

190

191

192

193

194

195

196

197

198

199

200

201

202

203

204

205

206

207

208

209

210

211

212

213

214

215

216

217

218

219

220

221

222

223

224

225

226

227

228

229

230

231

232

233

234

235

236

237

238

239

240

241

242

243

244

245

246

247

248

249

250

251

252

253

254

255

256

257

258

259

260

261

262

263

264

265

266

267

268

269

270

271

272

273

274

275

276

277

278

279

280

281

282

283

284

285

286

287

288

289

290

291

292

293

294

295

296

297

298

299

300

301

302

303

304

305

306

307

308

309

310

311

312

313

314

315

316

317

318

319

320

321

322

323

324

325

326

327

328

329

330

331

332

333

334

335

336

337

338

339

340

341

342

343

344

345

346

347

348

349

350

351

352

353

354

355

356

357

358

359

360

361

362

363

364

365
366
367
368
369
370
371
372
373
374
375
376
377
378
379
380
381
days

until

        finally

justice prevails.

SUMMER
1957

I.

I will not force my people to integrate against their will.
I will fight to preserve the rights guaranteed to the people under
the Constitution, and that includes control of the school—

Central High School
in Little Rock, Arkansas,

where nine Black students were

vetted
counseled
enrolled

to desegregate the South
&
test the ruling of
Brown v. Board of Education,

just to be tormented
day in
& day out,

all in the name of hope.

II.

armed soldiers
all around you

they line the sidewalks
surround you

everyone is yelling
screaming
in your ear

they better not let that nigger in here

someone spits on you

but you lift your head high
you won't dare let them see you cry

because you are

Elizabeth Eckford
you will be fine

because you are

one

of the

Little Rock Nine

Hazel Bryan hurls insults at Elizabeth Eckford, September 4, 1957.

III.

you stand tall
& think

*I'll go back
no matter what.*

the Civil Rights Act of 1957

was the *first* civil rights legislation since 1875, emphasizing
the right for ALL people to vote

& establishing

the Civil Rights section of the Justice Department.

H.R. 6127

proposed by President Dwight D. Eisenhower,
passed through Congress,

though not before it revised several key provisions,

like granting the ability to investigate
                    but not prosecute
citizens who denied or intimidated [Black] voters
at voting booths.

H.R. 6127, completely altered—

weak legislation, created by

strong opposition,

          appealing to

&   appeasing

the masses.

And so, Blacks marched for ~~better~~ equal rights . . .

and marched marched marched marched marched marched
marched marched marched marched marched marched
marched marched marched marched marched marched
marched marched marched marched marched marched
marched marched marched marched marched marched
marched marched marched marched marched marched
marched marched marched marched marched marched
marched marched marched

and marched marched marched marched marched marched
marched marched marched marched marched marched
marched marched marched marched marched marched
marched marched marched marched marched marched
marched marched marched marched marched marched
marched marched marched marched marched marched
marched marched marched marched marched marched
marched marched marched

and marched marched marched marched marched marched
marched marched marched marched marched marched
marched marched marched marched marched marched
marched marched marched marched marched marched
marched marched marched marched marched marched
marched marched marched marched marched marched
marched marched marched

and marched . . .

1959

MARCH 5

I.

welcome to another night
at the
Negro Boys Industrial School

tonight is no different
than any other night

you are
one
            of
                        sixty-nine
                                    boys
locked inside a room
withoutspace

one
            of
                                                sixty-nine
                                                boys
            who
                        shit
                        into buckets

                              beside their beds

one

         of

                              sixty-nine

                              boys

who were committed for the crimes of

              ~~theft~~

              ~~vandalism~~

              ~~truancy~~

              being Black

II.

you lie down
close your eyes
wake up

to

fire sweeping the ceiling
smoke filling the air

everyone starts

running
yelling
screaming

clawing at windows
clawing at each other

you escape through an opening

      barely

just in time
to see the building

c
　o
　　l
　　　l
　　　　a
　　　　　p
　　　　　s
　　　　　e

onto

　　　　bodies bodies bodies
　　　　bodies bodies bodies
　　　　bodies bodies bodies
　　　　bodies bodies bodies
　　　　bodies bodies bodies
　　　　bodies bodies bodies
　　　　bodies bodies bodies

　　　　　piled

　　one
　　atop
　　another

Black skin blackened
burned

to   bone

as

ashes blow over Wrightsville

III.

f r e e
at last

1960

the same people who mock

                             beat

         &   kill us

slather on sticky lotion

and fry their pale skin

outside

in the sun

inside

under a lamp

just to look dark

                             like us.

1961

MAY 14

I.

ride

or die

for there're things worse than death

       like being deprived of freedom

              until your last rattling breath

ride

or die

from Washington, D.C.,

       down to New Orleans

              to test a theory

ride

or die

by way of James Farmer's endorsement,

       he organized the Freedom Rides

              to challenge *Boynton v. Virginia*'s

              desegregation nonenforcement

ride
or die

on a rickety Greyhound
       thirteen brave souls
              headed southbound

ride
or die

when an armed mob arrives
       at a bus station, shouting
              burn them alive

ride
or die

when   windows are smashed
when   spirits are broken
when   tires are slashed

ride
or die

when a bomb is tossed inside
       smoke and flames, everywhere
              nowhere left to hide

ride
or die

after you make it out the door
      gasping for air
           only to be beaten and clubbed once more

ride
or die

after you crawl across the street
      coughing and bleeding
           refusing defeat

ride
or die

as a bullet cracks the air
      signaling the end
           of this "vigilante" affair

ride
or die

as the mob leaves the scene
      you lie in the grass, wondering
           is this all just a dream?

ride
or die

this will not be in vain
        four hundred more Freedom Riders
           you will gain

ride
or die

until they have no other choice
        but to listen to your demands
           to hear your steady voice

ride
or die

because, baby, this is war
        and victory will come justly
           but not 'til 1964

II.

break their spirit, not their bones
at Parchman Farm

where Freedom Riders were held, jailed

for

~~using "white" restrooms~~

trespassing
unlawful assembly
disorderly conduct

again

and again
    and again
        and again
            and again
                and again
                    and again
                        and again
                          and
                          again

neither slavery
nor involuntary servitude
except as a punishment
for crime whereof
the party shall have been duly convicted
shall exist within the United States
or any place subject to their jurisdiction

ha

what a lie

read the fine print

terms and conditions may apply

the thirteenth amendment

was supposed to set us free

grant us equal rights

and give us liberty

criminals—

that's what we are

for daring to exist

throw us all in jail

each time we try to resist

the shackles have been removed

yes, this is true

but, darling, we're still prisoners

of the red, white, and blue

locked up

behind   b b b b

a a a a

r r r r

s s s s

dr. king wrote a letter

he wanted to encourage everyone
to make America better

i am in Birmingham because injustice is here
we must act   now   without fear

freedom is never voluntarily given
it must be demanded by the oppressed
     this is the only road
       to guaranteed success

you express a great deal of anxiety
over our willingness to break laws
     you wouldn't
     if you've seen all the things I saw

for years now
I have heard the word   wait!

1.   (*v.*) a deceptive command

2.   (*n.*) a manufactured fate

we have waited
for more than 340 years
     drowning in our own
     blood, sweat, and tears

for our constitutional and God-given rights
     even now, we continue this fight

never before have I written so long a letter,
     (or should I say a book?)

so

do him a favor

Dr. King sits for a mugshot, Montgomery County, Alabama, February 21, 1956.

DR. KING WAS ARRESTED

on

January 26, 1956

    for

    speeding

on

March 22, 1956

    for

    organizing the Montgomery Bus Boycott

on

September 3, 1958

    for

    loitering

on

September 5, 1958

    for

    disobeying a police order

on

October 19, 1960

    for

    sitting in a restaurant

on

May 4, 1961

    for

    obstructing the sidewalk &

    parading without a permit

on

July 27, 1962

    for

    holding a prayer vigil

on

&

on

&

on

Dr. King was arrested,

    his body detained

    but never his spirit.

ON RARE OCCASIONS

between giving renowned speeches

&

being arrested 29 times

Dr. King loved to play pool,
                          his cue at the ready

                                    for the perfect shot.

    he loved listening to jazz, to revel in its
    triumphant organized chaos

    in our

    complicated urban existence.

                    . . . if only he had more
          free time.
                    if only he had more
          time . . .

. . . AND ON AND ON BLACKS MARCHED

and marched marched marched marched marched marched
marched marched marched marched marched marched
marched marched marched marched marched marched
marched marched marched marched marched marched
marched marched marched marched marched marched
marched marched marched marched marched marched
marched marched marched marched marched marched
marched marched marched

and marched marched marched marched marched marched
marched marched marched marched marched marched
marched marched marched marched marched marched
marched marched marched marched marched marched
marched marched marched marched marched marched
marched marched marched marched marched marched
marched marched marched marched marched marched
marched marched marched

and marched marched marched marched marched marched
marched marched marched marched marched marched
marched marched marched marched marched marched
marched marched marched marched marched marched
marched marched marched marched marched marched
marched marched marched marched marched marched
marched marched marched

and marched . . .

1963

MAY 11

I.

a cold jet of water

blasts you
with the force of a thousand bricks

and knocks you off your feet
as if you are nothing,

you're on the ground,
crawling
away . . .

                              away . . .

                                             away . . .

still,
they keep spraying,

as if you are   nothing . . .

II.

they release the dogs
your meat, a treat

for the animals they value
far more than you

                              but that was the plan,
all along . . .

III.

                    look at 'em run.
          I want to see the dogs work.

q: why . . . ? everyone asks.

why march? why dream? why fight? why die?

A protestor stands up to the water from a high-pressure fire hose in Birmingham, Alabama, 1963.

a: can't lose nothing . . .

ALL ARE FREE
OR NONE ARE!

Support Integration

UNION JUSTICE NOW!

GIVE US AMERICAN RIGHTS

JIM CROW
MUST GO

WE PROTEST
SCHOOL
SEGREGATION

VOTING RIGHTS *NOW!*

equal rights for all!

ASKING
DID NOT
WORK

RIGHTS
NOT
JAIL

. . . if you don't got nothing to lose.

1963

MAY 28

you sit at a greasy counter, feet touching
the sticky floor

people crowd you

pour coffee

in your hair

burn cigarettes

on your skin

dump sugar, ketchup, mustard

down your shirt

you stare past them
through watery eyes

thinking

we shall overcome
some   day

A white mob attacks sit-in protestors at
a lunch counter in Jackson, Mississippi.

hell—
might as well

flay our skin
peel back each layer

sheet
by
sheet

see for yourselves—
we're just like you

1963

AUGUST 28

arrive

    at the National Mall
    by ten, as planned

march   on Washington

    down Independence Avenue
    to the Lincoln Memorial
    with 250,000 people,   clapping
                                dancing
                                singing

    for change

sit

    under the late-summer sun,
    feet soaking in the Reflecting Pool,
    the water

a cool relief

listen

    to John Lewis
    wake up America

hear

Dr. King

share his dream . . .

at the greatest demonstration for freedom

in the history of our nation

Blacks and whites hold hands and sing during the March on Washington, Washington, D.C., August 28, 1963.

1963

SEPTEMBER 15

four
pleated dresses

four
sets of socks

four
pairs of shoes

four
beautiful girls

murdered
                              by the KKK
at
16th Street Baptist Church

on a quiet Sunday morning—

bibles and bodies,
bombed

if I could go back
i would capture the captors
and tell my people to flee

An African-American man breaks down during a
protest, Birmingham, Alabama, May 1963.

if I could go back
i would burn down the ships
so they never even crossed the sea

PART TWO

POWER TO THE PEOPLE

1964

APRIL 3

a ballot is like a bullet
Malcolm X said

hold Uncle Sam hostage
until "democracy" is dead

(MALCOLM) X

marked the spot
behind bars in Massachusetts   locked up
for six and a half years,

where he found a new faith and turned his life around,
flipped racist America   uʍop ǝpısdn
changed how we viewed civil rights,
used street knowledge to challenge the way we fight,

by denouncing nonviolence &

                                taking an active stance,
by returning the firepower   &

                                sticking it to the man.

                                      because
                          we were given freedom
                  but   we were never freed.

1964

JUNE 21

murder in Mississippi?

meh, nothing new

this time

> *a white man,*

> *a nigger,*

> *and a Jew*

An FBI poster seeking information on the
three missing civil rights activists.

kidnapped and driven to a secluded spot
all three activists, eventually shot

James Chaney
was to go first
breaking the buck
to quench the KKK's thirst

Michael Schwerner
took a bullet to the heart
he tried to explain
but they didn't let him start

Andrew Goodman
was buried alive
tried to claw his way out
but did not survive

all three bodies—covered with dirt
soon to be discovered—America, hurt

Edgar Ray Killen
caught a murder charge
the rest of the Klansmen—

somewhere at large

such a cliché   Southern tale

I wish I had a better story to
tell

                                    alas, my friend
                                    I have one final note
think twice before helping   Negroes
register to vote

THERE'S NO DIFFERENCE

between you

and I

except you get to live

and I get to die

trying

1964

JULY 2

the Civil Rights Act of 1964

BANNED

segregation
    &
    discrimination

in

    schools
    workplaces
    public spaces,

based on

    race
        color
    religion
        sex
        &
    national origin.

P.L. 88–352

proposed by

       John F. Kennedy,

signed by

       Lyndon B. Johnson,

prompted by

years & years

                of

             vengeance

        &   violence.

. . . and on and on Blacks marched

and marched marched marched marched marched marched
marched marched marched marched marched marched
marched marched marched marched marched marched
marched marched marched marched marched marched
marched marched marched marched marched marched
marched marched marched marched marched marched
marched marched marched marched marched marched
marched marched marched

and marched marched marched marched marched marched
marched marched marched marched marched marched
marched marched marched marched marched marched
marched marched marched marched marched marched
marched marched marched marched marched marched
marched marched marched marched marched marched
marched marched marched marched marched marched
marched marched marched

and marched marched marched marched marched marched
marched marched marched marched marched marched
marched marched marched marched marched marched
marched marched marched marched marched marched
marched marched marched marched marched marched
marched marched marched marched marched marched
marched marched marched

and marched . . .

1965

FEBRUARY 21

      X   X

        X   X

          X   X

malcolm   X   terminated

          X   X

        X   X

      X   X

negro, *noun.*

neither African
nor American

just the hated love child
of liberty and death

A member of the American Nazi Party, protesting desegregation, 1965.

1965

MARCH 7

stand fearless   this Bloody Sunday,
                                  with 600 people
against a wall of state troopers
here, on the Grand Dragon's bridge—

your presence, an insult
to their shrine

stay put
as they secure their gas masks

don't flinch
when they rush forward

don't cry
after they knock you down

let them
            beat you in the head
            with billy clubs

let them
            trample your body
            to reach another

as you lie unconscious, breathing in
tear gas

over the swirling waters

of the Alabama River

Police officers corner a civil rights marcher on the Edmund Pettus
Bridge in Selma, Alabama, 1965.

THIS IS LIFE—

years of bloodshed
but they still don't consider you
                                    human

1965

MARCH 17

Democrats and Republicans
introduce a bill
to secure African-Americans
the—federal—right to vote

by eliminating
       literacy tests,
       the Grandfather Clause,
&   the poll tax

for good.

No longer will Blacks have to

hunt for spare change,
wonder if they will be asked to recite
the entire Constitution from memory,
wish they were a legalized exception,

thanks to

S. 1564, signed
into law, on
August 6, by

Lyndon B. Johnson

—finally
a true act of

equality.

1966

JUNE 16

on this day
        in the *Cotton Capital of the World*

Stokely Carmichael never meant
for **BLACK POWER!** to be a threat

just a call for us to love—

        nappy hair
        wide noses
        full lips
        dark(er) skin

—everything they convinced us to hate

a call for us to redefine ourselves
by defining ourselves   with our own definitions

yet

people fear(ed) words
        fear(ed) *us*
more than weapons

1966

SEPTEMBER 27

I.

Matthew Johnson
an unarmed Black teenager
k i l l e d
by a white patrol officer
in 1966

for
joyriding with two friends

the car, stolen
the officer, in pursuit

Matthew Johnson
shot in the back
while fleeing
for his life

four bullets   fired
without hesitation

one

into his heart

Matthew Johnson
lying facedown, bleeding
in the streets
of San Francisco

dead

never given the chance
to stand trial for his crimes

      the fourteenth amendment—
      disregarded

because the only thing worse than a criminal
is a Black criminal

Matthew Johnson,
his murder ruled
a justifiable homicide

the officer, a hero
reinstated to the force
from his   *suspension without pay*

Matthew Johnson

an example

his-story

history

to be repeated repeated repeated repeated repeated
repeated repeated repeated repeated repeated repeated
repeated repeated repeated repeated repeated repeated
repeated repeated repeated repeated repeated repeated
repeated repeated repeated repeated repeated repeated
repeated repeated repeated repeated

II.

the residents of Hunters Point, no longer quiet,
took to the streets, started a riot

talked of storming the police station
in their eyes, a citizen's obligation

the governor met their fire with fire
martial law imposed; the situation, dire

this uprising
foreshadowed America's fate
for justice—people would no longer wait

Matthew Johnson, a martyr
in heaven

battles raged in his name
until 1967

RETROSPECT IS A PLACE

where the truth lives

guilt free

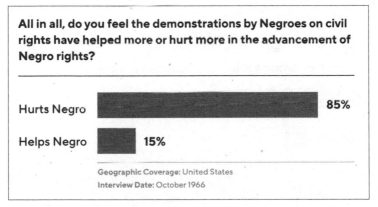

All in all, do you feel the demonstrations by Negroes on civil rights have helped more or hurt more in the advancement of Negro rights?

Hurts Negro — 85%

Helps Negro — 15%

Geographic Coverage: United States
Interview Date: October 1966

Survey results of white Americans when asked their opinion on civil rights demonstrations led by Blacks, October 1966.

the Black Panther Party formed
a ten-point program

to serve the community—free breakfast for children,
free healthcare for families

and to
police the police

by
marching around neighborhoods, in uniform
exercising their second amendment rights

to defend

black pride
black power

too much power

a communist organization
an FBI target

Fred Hampton

gunned down
in his sleep

Angela Davis
on the run,
WANTED

for ~~educating the masses~~ aggravated kidnapping
and first-degree murder

later captured
later freed

the greatest threat to the internal security of the country—

the Black Panther Party—
later dissolved

. . . and on and on Blacks marched

and marched marched marched marched marched marched
marched marched marched marched marched marched
marched marched marched marched marched marched
marched marched marched marched marched marched
marched marched marched marched marchedmarched
marched marched marched marched marched marched
marched marched marched marched marched marched
marched marched marched

and marched marched marched marched marched marched
marched marched marched marched marched marched
marched marched marched marched marched marched
marched marched marched marched marched marched
marched marched marched marched marched marched
marched marched marched marched marched marched
marched marched marched marched marched marched
marched marched marched

and marched marched marched marched marched marched
marched marched marched marched marched marched
marched marched marched marched marched marched
marched marched marched marched marched marched
marched marched marched marched marched marched
marched marched marched marched marched marched
marched marched marched

and marched . . .

PART THREE

THE BEGINNING OF THE END

1968

FEBRUARY 1

I.

rain falls
in sheets
across   Memphis, Tennessee,

              too bad
          sanitation workers

keep   on   truckin'
along those slick city streets

because—

              too bad—
garbage
doesn't collect itself

too bad

Echol Cole   and Robert Walker
climb inside the rusty barrel

of   their dump on wheels

and stand beside

      leaky tubs of human waste

      (finally! warmth!)

too bad
the machinery malfunctions

too bad
two men

are swallowed whole

too bad
their skulls are crushed

their brains

         s

                 c

          a

      t

                       t

                   e

            r

     e

 d

across the filth

like stringy pieces of uncooked beef

too bad . . .

II.

men, in suits

wearing

I <u>AM</u> A MAN

sandwich boards

walking

the dirty streets
of Memphis, Tennessee,

on strike

wondering

3/5 of a man,
am I
still?

III.

stank

                                               everywhere

soiled diapers
spoiled meat

plastic
metal
glass

all over the streets, all over the sidewalks

everywhere you step,

trash

no Black people
no sanitation workers
       to clean it all up

. . . and on and on Blacks marched

and marched marched marched marched marched marched
marchedmarched marched marched marched marched
marched marched marched marched marched marched
marched marched marched marched marched marched
marched marched marched marched marched marched
marched marched marched marched marched marched
marched marched marched marched marched marched
marched marched marched marched marched marched
marched marched marched

and marched marched marched marched marched marched
marched marched marched marched marched marched
marched marched marched marched marched marched
marched marched marched marched marched marched
marched marched marched marched marched marched
marched marched marched marched marched marched
marched marched marched marched marched marched
marched marched marched

and marched marched marched marched marched marched
marched marched marched marched marched marched
marched marched marched marched marched marched
marched marched marched marched marched marched
marched marched marched marched marched marched
marched marched marched marched marched marched
marched marched marched marched marched marched
marched marched marched

and marched . . .

1968

APRIL 4

I.

at

6:01 p.m.

a .30-06

pierced
Dr. King's cheek

shattering
his jaw

severing
his spine

necktie ripped off,
he

dropped

7:05 p.m.

dead

I remember when they told me Dr. King had been killed.
I remember falling on my knees. Falling out, crying.
I can remember I was in the den, all of us,
crying.

II.

O King of kings!
it is just as you said
like our dear Captain
you've fallen cold and dead
>> on the deck
>>>> of the Lorraine Motel
>>>> Memphis, Tennessee,
>>>> your final farewell

O King of kings!
so gracious and fair
to the Mason Temple kingdom
we watched you declare
>> a royal proclamation
>>>> from your mountaintop throne
>>>> that we'd get to the Promised Land
>>>> but we'd get there alone

O King of kings!
we rise, dying, to overthrow the Divine Right
your noble court, loyal
carrying on the fight
>> for His Majesty has moved on
>>>> his peaceful legacy slain
>>>> but little do they know
>>>> that We, the People, will reign

III.

Dr. King said
a riot is the language of the unheard

and so
      America screamed

for him

windows, smashed
buildings, burned

the National Guard, summoned

43 people
      dead
200 cities
      destroyed
3,500 survivors
      injured
27,000 civilians
      arrested
58,000 soldiers
      deployed

1 bill

signed

Troops patrol Washington, D.C., after the assassination of Dr. Martin Luther King Jr.

—the final Civil Rights Act,
a new law
a victory

born from violence
all for fair housing.

1954 to 1968

death was everywhere
then.

now

when we speak of those events
we speak of them so casually,

as if four little girls weren't blown to bits,
their limbs scattered across the church floor,

four less niggers.

we speak as if Klansmen weren't bombing Black
homes
in the middle of the night,

all because a Black man dared to register to vote.

we forget to remember
the true horrors
of our past

and speak
as if Black lives ran

natural courses,
not as if they were hunted down

and murdered,

by   silence
     compliance

     approval

for "traditions" to live on
     and

     repeat.

AFTERWORD

history has become
a beautiful American lie
Overseers rewrite it
and always deny

people the right
to know the ugly truth
only tell part of it
especially to the youth

peace peace peace
they always insist
while lawmakers attempt to
cease and desist

the full story
from impressionable minds
there's no better way
to keep everyone in line

from the Civil War
to civil rights
they'll never stop downplaying
the brutality of our fights

so now you know
some of the things they keep from you
I can only hope
you'll spread the knowledge, too

because there's one way
to set everyone free
it starts with making a difference
it starts with you and me

AUTHOR'S NOTE

A few years ago, I was scrolling down my Facebook News Feed and saw a post about Rosa Parks. I read that she wasn't the first Black woman to refuse her seat to a white passenger—Claudette Colvin was. My jaw dropped. Why hadn't I heard of Claudette Colvin before? Why wasn't she in (m)any history books? What else was I not being told?

As it turns out, there were many things I didn't know. For example: Dr. King was as hated in his time (by white people) as Colin Kaepernick is hated in this time (also by white people). That the Civil Rights Acts were passed after days, weeks, years of unfortunate violence—not peaceful marches that went largely ignored.

So, I started searching for the truth—the *full* truth. I asked people who lived through it all (among them my mother and grandmother). I combed through (auto)biographies and memoirs. I looked through museum galleries, in person and online. I discovered many heartbreaking things, some of which I've shared here with you. There is still so much to learn. Still so much to share.

I wrote this poetry collection to place readers in that tragic era. To expose the truth—the full truth—and nothing less. Because, as Dr. King once said, "We are not makers of history. We are made by history." Together, we can make the world a better place, made by the history of today.

ACKNOWLEDGMENTS

Mom—for believing in me, always. Forever.

Family—for cheering me on from the very start.

Kandace—for reading everything I send you, no matter what.

Rena—for being a freakin' rock star. Seriously.

Liza—for fighting so hard for this collection and for your otherworldly vision to see its potential beyond anything I could've ever imagined.

Krisann—for being the best critique partner, like, ever.

TIMELINE

May 17, 1954

Segregation in public schools is ruled unconstitutional in *Brown v. Board of Education.*

August 28, 1955

Emmett Till is murdered in Money, Mississippi.

December 1, 1955

Rosa Parks refuses to give up her seat on a bus in Montgomery, Alabama.

December 5, 1955

The Montgomery Bus Boycott begins.

August 26, 1956

The Clinton 12 become the first African-American students to integrate a public school in the South (Clinton, Tennessee): Jo Ann Boyce (née Allen), Bobby Cain, Theresser Caswell, Minnie Ann Jones (née Dickey), Gail Ann Upton (née Epps), Ronald Hayden, William Latham, Alvah J. Lambert (née McSwain), Maurice Soles, Robert Thacker, Regina Smith (née Turner), and Alfred Williams.

December 20, 1956

The Montgomery Bus Boycott ends.

September 4, 1957

The Little Rock Nine become the second group of African-American students to challenge racial segregation in public schools (Little Rock, Arkansas): Minnijean Brown, Elizabeth

Eckford, Ernest Green, Thelma Mothershed, Melba Patillo, Gloria Ray, Terrence Roberts, Jefferson Thomas, and Carlotta Walls.

September 9, 1957

The Civil Rights Act of 1957 is signed into law.

March 5, 1959

The Negro Boys Industrial School catches fire in Wrightsville, Arkansas, claiming the lives of twenty-one teenage boys: Carl E. Thornton, Cecil Preston, Charles L. Thomas, Charles White, Edward Tolston Jr., Frank Barnes, Amos Gyce, Henry Daniels, Jessie Carpenter Jr., Joe Crittenden, John Alfred George, John Daniel, Johnnie Tillison, Lindsey Cross, O. T. Meadows, R. D. Brown, Roy Chester Powell, Roy Hegwood, William Piggee, Willie G. Horner, and Willie Lee Williams.

Very few people were even aware of the school's existence before this tragedy took place. The fire made the front pages of several local and nonlocal papers, but nothing was ever done. No one was ever prosecuted.

February 1, 1960

The Greensboro sit-ins begin (Greensboro, North Carolina): David Richmond, Ezell Blair Jr., Franklin McCain, and Joseph McNeil—the Greensboro Four.

May 14, 1961

The KKK attacks two buses full of Freedom Riders: James Farmer, James Peck, Genevieve Hughes, Joe Perkins, Walter Bergman, Frances Bergman, Albert Bigelow, Jimmy McDonald, Ed Blankenheim, Hank Thomas, Charles Person, Rev. Benjamin Elton Cox, and John Lewis.

April 16, 1963

Dr. King pens "Letter from a Birmingham Jail" while incarcerated.

August 28, 1963

The March on Washington for Jobs and Freedom takes place.

September 15, 1963

The KKK bombs 16th Street Baptist Church, killing four African-American girls: Addie Mae Collins, Denise McNair, Carole Robertson, and Cynthia Wesley.

April 3, 1964

Malcolm X delivers his famous "The Ballot or the Bullet" speech at Cory Methodist Church in Cleveland, Ohio.

June 21, 1964

The KKK kidnaps and kills three civil rights activists: James Chaney, Andrew Goodman, and Michael Schwerner.

July 2, 1964

The Civil Rights Act of 1964 is signed into law.

February 21, 1965

Malcolm X is assassinated.

March 7, 1965

The first Selma to Montgomery march ends in "Bloody Sunday."

August 6, 1965

The Voting Rights Act is signed into law.

June 16, 1966

Stokely Carmichael founds the Black Power movement at a protest rally in Greenwood, Mississippi.

September 27, 1966

A white patrol officer shoots and kills unarmed Black teenager

Matthew Johnson in San Francisco, California, sparking the Hunters Point Uprising.

October 15, 1966

Huey Newton and Bobby Seale found the Black Panther Party.

February 12, 1968

The Memphis Sanitation Workers' Strike begins.

April 3, 1968

Dr. Martin Luther King Jr. delivers his last speech: "I've Been to the Mountaintop."

April 4, 1968

Dr. Martin Luther King Jr. is assassinated at the Lorraine Motel in Memphis, Tennessee.

April 11, 1968

The final Civil Rights Act is signed into law.

SOURCES

- "inherently unequal": the Supreme Court unanimously declaring legal segregation as an unconstitutional violation of the Fourteenth Amendment in *Brown v. Board of Education*, May 17, 1954

- "a great day for America and its court": Justice Harold H. Burton to Chief Justice Earl Warren, May 17, 1954, concerning Warren's decision in *Brown v. Board of Education*, Earl Warren Papers, Manuscript Division, Library of Congress

- "get up": Claudette Colvin quoting what the bus driver commanded her to do in *Claudette Colvin: Twice toward Justice* by Phillip Hoose (New York: Farrar Straus Giroux, 2014), page 32

- "I paid my fare, it's my constitutional right!": Claudette Colvin quoting what she told bus driver in *Claudette Colvin: Twice toward Justice* by Phillip Hoose, page 32

- "nigger bitch": Claudette Colvin quoting what two cops called her during her ride to the police station in *Claudette Colvin: Twice toward Justice* by Phillip Hoose, page 32

- "three bare walls, a toilet, and a cot": Claudette Colvin describing her jail cell, quoted in *Claudette Colvin: Twice toward Justice* by Phillip Hoose, page 34

- "their ashes blew over Wrightsville": Frank Lawrence's (brother of Lindsey Cross) statement quoted in "Stirring the Ashes" by Leslie Newell Peacock, *Arkansas Times*, February 29, 2008, https://arktimes.com/news/cover-stories/2008/02/29/stirring-the-ashes-2

- "burn them alive": armed white mob screaming at a bus full of Freedom Riders, as quoted in *Freedom Riders: 1961 and the Struggle for Racial Justice* by Raymond Arsenault (New York: Oxford University Press, 2011), page 97

- "break their spirit, not their bones": governor of Mississippi, Ross Barnett, instructions regarding the Freedom Riders' safety, as detailed in *Worse than Slavery: Parchman Farm and the Ordeal of Jim Crow Justice* by David M. Oshinsky (New York: Free Press, 1997), page 235

- "coughing and bleeding": description of the bus bombing aftermath, as quoted in *Freedom Riders: 1961 and the Struggle for Racial Justice* by Raymond Arsenault, page 98

- "the greatest demonstration for freedom in the history of our nation": Dr. Martin Luther King Jr., "I Have a Dream," August 28, 1963, the March on Washington for Jobs and Freedom, the Martin Luther King, Jr. Research and Education Institute, Stanford University, https://kinginstitute .stanford.edu/king-papers/documents/i-have-dream -address-delivered-march-washington-jobs-and-freedom

- "a ballot is like a bullet": Malcolm X, "The Ballot or the Bullet," April 3, 1964, Cory Methodist Church, Cleveland, Ohio

- "a riot is the language of the unheard": Dr. Martin Luther King Jr. "The Other America," April 14, 1967, Stanford University, https://kinginstitute.stanford.edu/news/50-years -ago-martin-luther-king-jr-speaks-stanford-university

- "they killed one nigger, one Jew, and a white man": Judge William Harold Cox during the Mississippi Burning Trial, October 1967, https://www.fbi.gov/history/famous-cases /mississippi-burning

- "the greatest threat to the internal security of the country": former FBI director J. Edgar Hoover regarding the Black Panther Party, July 16, 1969, in the FBI's annual report for the 1969 fiscal year

- "you've fallen cold and dead": Walt Whitman, "O Captain! My Captain!" in *Leaves of Grass: The Complete 1855 and 1891–92 Editions* (New York: Library of America, 2011), page 467

- "All you gotta do is tell them you're going to bring the dogs. Look at 'em run. I want to see the dogs work.": Eugene "Bull" Connor, police chief of Birmingham, Alabama, May 1963

- "I will not force my people to integrate against their will. I will fight to preserve the rights guaranteed to the people under the Constitution, and that includes control of the school.": Governor Orval Faubus, "Speech on School Integration," 1958

- "I'll go back no matter what.": Minnijean Brown-Trickey's statement quoted in "Little Rock Nine: The Day Young Students Shattered Racial Segregation" by David Smith, the *Guardian*, September 24, 2017, https://www.theguardian.com/world/2017/sep/24/little-rock-arkansas-school-segregation-racism

- "I remember when they told me Dr. King had been killed. I remember falling on my knees. Falling out, crying. I can remember I was in the den, all of us, crying.": Hal Martin, an African-American woman who marched with Dr. King and lived through the Civil Rights Movement

- "People always say that I didn't give up my seat because I was tired, but that isn't true. I was not tired physically, or no more tired than I usually was at the end of a working day. I was not old, although some people have an image of me as being old then. I was forty-two. No, the only tired I was, was tired of giving in.": Rosa Parks, in *Rosa Parks: My Story* with Jim Haskins (New York: Puffin Books, 1999), page 116

- "four less niggers": white supremacist leader Connie Lynch, regarding the 16th Street Baptist Church bombing, as detailed in *Free at Last: A History of the Civil Rights Movement and Those Who Died in the Struggle* by Sarah Bullard (New York: Oxford University Press, 1993), page 63

- "Letter from a Birmingham Jail": African Studies Center at University of Pennsylvania, https://www.africa.upenn.edu /Articles_Gen/Letter_Birmingham.html, page 61

IMAGE CREDITS

FURTHER READING

Alexander, Michelle. *The New Jim Crow: Mass Incarceration in the Age of Colorblindness*. 10th Anniversary Edition. New York: New Press, 2020.

Allen Boyce, Jo Ann, and Debbie Levy. *This Promise of Change: One Girl's Story in the Fight for School Equality*. New York: Bloomsbury Children's Books, 2019.

Arsenault, Raymond. *Freedom Riders: 1961 and the Struggle for Racial Justice*. New York: Oxford University Press, 2011.

Goldstone, Lawrence, with foreword by Henry Louis Gates Jr. *Stolen Justice: The Struggle for African American Voting Rights*. New York: Scholastic Focus, 2020.

Hoose, Phillip. *Claudette Colvin: Twice toward Justice*. New York: Farrar, Straus and Giroux, 2014.

Reynolds, Jason. *Stamped: Racism, Antiracism, and You: A Remix of the National Book Award-Winning Stamped from the Beginning*. New York: Little, Brown, 2020.

Stockley, Grif. *Black Boys Burning: The 1959 Fire at the Arkansas Negro Boys Industrial School*. Jackson: University Press of Mississippi, 2017.

Woodson, Jacqueline. *Brown Girl Dreaming*. New York: Puffin Books, 2014.

BONUS CONTENT

"Letter from a Birmingham Jail"
Martin Luther King Jr.

16 April 1963

My Dear Fellow Clergymen:

While confined here in the Birmingham city jail, I came across your recent statement calling my present activities "unwise and untimely." Seldom do I pause to answer criticism of my work and ideas. If I sought to answer all the criticisms that cross my desk, my secretaries would have little time for anything other than such correspondence in the course of the day, and I would have no time for constructive work. But since I feel that you are men of genuine good will and that your criticisms are sincerely set forth, I want to try to answer your statement in what I hope will be patient and reasonable terms.

I think I should indicate why I am here in Birmingham, since you have been influenced by the view which argues against "outsiders coming in." I have the honor of serving as president of the Southern Christian Leadership Conference, an organization operating in every southern state, with headquarters in Atlanta, Georgia. We have some eighty-five affiliated organizations across the South, and one of them is the Alabama Christian Movement for Human Rights. Frequently we share staff, educational and financial resources with our affiliates. Several months ago the affiliate here in Birmingham asked us to be on call to engage in a nonviolent direct action program if such were deemed necessary. We readily consented, and when the hour came we lived up to our promise. So I, along with several members of my staff, am here because I was invited here. I am here because I have organizational ties here.

But more basically, I am in Birmingham because injustice is here. Just as the prophets of the eighth century B.C. left their villages and carried their "thus saith the Lord" far beyond the boundaries of their home towns, and just as the Apostle Paul left his village of Tarsus and carried the gospel of

Jesus Christ to the far corners of the Greco Roman world, so am I compelled to carry the gospel of freedom beyond my own home town. Like Paul, I must constantly respond to the Macedonian call for aid.

Moreover, I am cognizant of the interrelatedness of all communities and states. I cannot sit idly by in Atlanta and not be concerned about what happens in Birmingham. Injustice anywhere is a threat to justice everywhere. We are caught in an inescapable network of mutuality, tied in a single garment of destiny. Whatever affects one directly, affects all indirectly. Never again can we afford to live with the narrow, provincial "outside agitator" idea. Anyone who lives inside the United States can never be considered an outsider anywhere within its bounds.

You deplore the demonstrations taking place in Birmingham. But your statement, I am sorry to say, fails to express a similar concern for the conditions that brought about the demonstrations. I am sure that none of you would want to rest content with the superficial kind of social analysis that deals merely with effects and does not grapple with underlying causes. It is unfortunate that demonstrations are taking place in Birmingham, but it is even more unfortunate that the city's white power structure left the Negro community with no alternative.

In any nonviolent campaign there are four basic steps: collection of the facts to determine whether injustices exist; negotiation; self purification; and direct action. We have gone through all these steps in Birmingham. There can be no gainsaying the fact that racial injustice engulfs this community. Birmingham is probably the most thoroughly segregated city in the United States. Its ugly record of brutality is widely known. Negroes have experienced grossly unjust treatment in the courts. There have been more unsolved bombings of Negro homes and churches in Birmingham than in any other city in the nation. These are the hard, brutal facts of the case. On the basis of these conditions, Negro leaders sought to negotiate with the city fathers. But the latter consistently refused to engage in good faith negotiation.

Then, last September, came the opportunity to talk with leaders of Birmingham's economic community. In the course of the negotiations, certain promises were made by the merchants—for example, to remove the stores' humiliating racial signs. On the basis of these promises, the Reverend Fred Shuttlesworth and the leaders of the Alabama Christian Movement for Human Rights agreed to a moratorium on all demonstrations. As the weeks and months went by, we realized that we were the victims of a broken promise. A few signs, briefly removed, returned; the others remained. As in so many past experiences, our hopes had been blasted, and the shadow of deep disappointment settled upon us. We had no alternative except to prepare for direct action, whereby we would present our very bodies as a means of laying our case before the conscience of the local and the national community. Mindful of the difficulties involved, we decided to undertake a process of self purification. We began a series of workshops on nonviolence, and we repeatedly asked ourselves: "Are you able to accept blows without retaliating?" "Are you able to endure the ordeal of jail?" We decided to schedule our direct action program for the Easter season, realizing that except for Christmas, this is the main shopping period of the year. Knowing that a strong economic-withdrawal program would be the by product of direct action, we felt that this would be the best time to bring pressure to bear on the merchants for the needed change.

Then it occurred to us that Birmingham's mayoral election was coming up in March, and we speedily decided to postpone action until after election day. When we discovered that the Commissioner of Public Safety, Eugene "Bull" Connor, had piled up enough votes to be in the runoff, we decided again to postpone action until the day after the run off so that the demonstrations could not be used to cloud the issues. Like many others, we waited to see Mr. Connor defeated, and to this end we endured postponement after postponement. Having aided in this community need, we felt that our direct action program could be delayed no longer.

You may well ask: "Why direct action? Why sit ins, marches and so forth? Isn't negotiation a better path?" You are quite right in calling for negotiation. Indeed, this is the very purpose of direct action. Nonviolent direct action seeks to create such a crisis and foster such a tension that a community which has constantly refused to negotiate is forced to confront the issue. It seeks so to dramatize the issue that it can no longer be ignored. My citing the creation of tension as part of the work of the nonviolent resister may sound rather shocking. But I must confess that I am not afraid of the word "tension." I have earnestly opposed violent tension, but there is a type of constructive, nonviolent tension which is necessary for growth. Just as Socrates felt that it was necessary to create a tension in the mind so that individuals could rise from the bondage of myths and half truths to the unfettered realm of creative analysis and objective appraisal, so must we see the need for nonviolent gadflies to create the kind of tension in society that will help men rise from the dark depths of prejudice and racism to the majestic heights of understanding and brotherhood. The purpose of our direct action program is to create a situation so crisis packed that it will inevitably open the door to negotiation. I therefore concur with you in your call for negotiation. Too long has our beloved Southland been bogged down in a tragic effort to live in monologue rather than dialogue.

One of the basic points in your statement is that the action that I and my associates have taken in Birmingham is untimely. Some have asked: "Why didn't you give the new city administration time to act?" The only answer that I can give to this query is that the new Birmingham administration must be prodded about as much as the outgoing one, before it will act. We are sadly mistaken if we feel that the election of Albert Boutwell as mayor will bring the millennium to Birmingham. While Mr. Boutwell is a much more gentle person than Mr. Connor, they are both segregationists, dedicated to maintenance of the status quo. I have hope that Mr. Boutwell will be reasonable enough to see the futility of massive resistance to desegregation. But he will not see this without pressure from devotees of civil rights. My friends, I must say to you that we have not made a single gain in civil rights without determined legal and nonviolent pressure. Lamentably, it is an historical fact that privileged groups seldom give up their privileges voluntarily. Individuals may see the moral light and voluntarily give up their unjust posture; but, as Reinhold Niebuhr has reminded us, groups tend to be more immoral than individuals.

We know through painful experience that freedom is never voluntarily given by the oppressor; it must be demanded by the oppressed. Frankly, I have yet to engage in a direct action campaign that was "well timed" in the view of those who have not suffered unduly from the disease of segregation. For years now I have heard the word "Wait!" It rings in the ear of every Negro with piercing familiarity. This "Wait" has almost always meant "Never." We must come to see, with one of our distinguished jurists, that "justice too long delayed is justice denied."

We have waited for more than 340 years for our constitutional and God given rights. The nations of Asia and Africa are moving with jetlike speed toward gaining political independence, but we still creep at horse and buggy pace toward gaining a cup of coffee at a lunch counter. Perhaps it is easy for those who have never felt the stinging darts of segregation to say, "Wait." But when you have seen vicious mobs lynch your mothers and fathers at will and drown your sisters and brothers at whim; when you have seen hate filled policemen curse, kick and even kill your black brothers and sisters; when you see the vast majority of your twenty million Negro brothers smothering in an airtight cage of poverty in the midst of an affluent society; when you suddenly find your tongue twisted and your speech stammering as you seek to explain to your six year old daughter why she can't go to the public amusement park that has just been advertised on television, and see tears welling up in her eyes when she is told that Funtown is closed to colored children, and see ominous clouds of inferiority beginning to form in her little mental sky, and see her beginning to distort her personality by developing an unconscious bitterness toward white people; when you have to concoct an answer for a five year old son who is asking: "Daddy, why do white people treat colored people so mean?"; when you take a cross county drive and find it necessary to sleep night after night in the uncomfortable corners of your automobile because no motel will accept you; when you are humiliated day in and day out by nagging signs reading "white" and "colored"; when your first name becomes "nigger," your middle name becomes "boy" (however old you are) and your last name becomes "John," and your wife and mother are never given the respected title "Mrs."; when you are harried by day and haunted by night by the fact that you are a Negro, living constantly at tiptoe stance, never quite knowing what to expect next, and are plagued with inner fears and outer resentments; when you are forever fighting a degenerating sense of "nobodiness"—then you will understand why we find it difficult to wait. There comes a time when the cup of endurance runs over, and men are no longer willing to be plunged into the abyss of despair. I hope, sirs, you can understand our legitimate and unavoidable impatience. You express a great deal of anxiety over our willingness to break laws. This is certainly a legitimate concern. Since we so diligently urge people to obey the Supreme Court's decision of 1954 outlawing segregation in the public schools, at first glance it may seem rather paradoxical for us consciously to break laws. One may well ask: "How can you advocate breaking some laws and obeying others?" The answer lies in the fact that there are two types of laws: just and unjust. I would be the first to advocate obeying just laws. One has not only a legal but a moral responsibility to obey just laws. Conversely, one has a moral responsibility to disobey unjust laws. I would agree with St. Augustine that "an unjust law is no law at all."

Now, what is the difference between the two? How does one determine whether a law is just or unjust? A just law is a man made code that squares with the moral law or the law of God. An unjust law is a code that is out of harmony with the moral law. To put it in the terms of St. Thomas Aquinas: An unjust law is a human law that is not rooted in eternal law and natural law. Any law that uplifts human personality is just. Any law that degrades human personality is unjust. All segregation statutes are unjust because segregation distorts the soul and damages the personality. It gives the segregator a false sense of superiority and the segregated a false sense of inferiority. Segregation, to use the terminology of the Jewish philosopher Martin Buber, substitutes an "I it" relationship for an "I thou" relationship and ends up relegating persons to the status of things. Hence segregation is not only politically, economically and sociologically unsound, it is morally wrong and sinful. Paul Tillich has said that sin is separation. Is not segregation an existential expression of man's tragic separation, his awful estrangement, his terrible sinfulness? Thus it is that I can urge men to obey the 1954 decision of the Supreme Court, for it is morally right; and I can urge them to disobey segregation ordinances, for they are morally wrong.

Let us consider a more concrete example of just and unjust laws. An unjust law is a code that a numerical or power majority group compels a minority group to obey but does not make binding on itself. This is difference made legal. By the same token, a just law is a code that a majority compels a minority to follow and that it is willing to follow itself. This is sameness made legal. Let me give another explanation. A law is unjust if it is inflicted on a minority that, as a result of being denied the right to vote, had no part in enacting or devising the law. Who can say that the legislature of Alabama which set up that state's segregation laws was democratically elected? Throughout Alabama all sorts of devious methods are used to prevent Negroes from becoming registered voters, and there are some counties in which, even though Negroes constitute a majority of the population, not a single Negro is registered. Can any law enacted under such circumstances be considered democratically structured?

Sometimes a law is just on its face and unjust in its application. For instance, I have been arrested on a charge of parading without a permit. Now, there is nothing wrong in having an ordinance which requires a permit for a parade. But such an ordinance becomes unjust when it is used to maintain segregation and to deny citizens the First-Amendment privilege of peaceful assembly and protest.

I hope you are able to see the distinction I am trying to point out. In no sense do I advocate evading or defying the law, as would the rabid segregationist. That would lead to anarchy. One who breaks an unjust law must do so openly, lovingly, and with a willingness to accept the penalty. I submit that an individual who breaks a law that conscience tells him is unjust, and who willingly accepts the penalty of imprisonment in order to arouse the conscience of the community over its injustice, is in reality expressing the highest respect for law.

Of course, there is nothing new about this kind of civil disobedience. It was evidenced sublimely in the refusal of Shadrach, Meshach and Abednego to obey the laws of Nebuchadnezzar, on the ground that a higher moral law was at stake. It was practiced superbly by the early Christians, who were willing to face hungry lions and the excruciating pain of chopping blocks rather than submit to certain unjust laws of the Roman Empire. To a degree, academic freedom is a reality today because Socrates practiced civil disobedience. In our own nation, the Boston Tea Party represented a massive act of civil disobedience.

We should never forget that everything Adolf Hitler did in Germany was "legal" and everything the Hungarian freedom fighters did in Hungary was "illegal." It was "illegal" to aid and comfort a Jew in Hitler's Germany. Even so, I am sure that, had I lived in Germany at the time, I would have aided and comforted my Jewish brothers. If today I lived in a Communist country where certain principles dear to the Christian faith are suppressed, I would openly advocate disobeying that country's antireligious laws.

I must make two honest confessions to you, my Christian and Jewish brothers. First, I must confess that over the past few years I have been gravely disappointed with the white moderate. I have almost reached the regrettable conclusion that the Negro's great stumbling block in his stride toward freedom is not the White Citizen's Counciler or the Ku Klux Klanner, but the white moderate, who is more devoted to "order" than to justice; who prefers a negative peace which is the absence of tension to a positive peace which is the presence of justice; who constantly says: "I agree with you in the goal you seek, but I cannot agree with your methods of direct action"; who paternalistically believes he can set the timetable for another man's freedom; who lives by a mythical concept of time and who constantly advises the Negro to wait for a "more convenient season." Shallow understanding from people of good will is more frustrating than absolute misunderstanding from people of ill will. Lukewarm acceptance is much more bewildering than outright rejection.

I had hoped that the white moderate would understand that law and order exist for the purpose of establishing justice and that when they fail in this purpose they become the dangerously structured dams that block the flow of social progress. I had hoped that the white moderate would understand that the present tension in the South is a necessary phase of the transition from an obnoxious negative peace, in which the Negro passively accepted his unjust plight, to a substantive and positive peace, in which all men will respect the dignity and worth of human personality. Actually, we who engage in nonviolent direct action are not the creators of tension. We merely bring to the surface the hidden tension that is already alive. We bring it out in the open, where it can be seen and dealt with. Like a boil that can never be cured so long as it is covered up but must be opened with all its ugliness to the natural medicines of air and light, injustice must be exposed, with all the tension its exposure creates, to the light of human conscience and the air of national opinion before it can be cured.

In your statement you assert that our actions, even though peaceful, must be condemned because they precipitate violence. But is this a logical assertion? Isn't this like condemning a robbed man because his possession of money precipitated the evil act of robbery? Isn't this like condemning Socrates because his unswerving commitment to truth and his philosophical inquiries precipitated the act by the misguided populace in which they made him drink hemlock? Isn't this like condemning Jesus because his unique God consciousness and never ceasing devotion to God's will precipitated the evil act of crucifixion? We must come to see that, as the federal courts have consistently affirmed, it is wrong to urge an individual to cease his efforts to gain his basic constitutional rights because the quest may precipitate violence. Society must protect the robbed and punish the robber. I had also hoped that the white moderate would reject the myth concerning time in relation to the struggle for freedom. I have just received a letter from a white brother in Texas. He writes: "All Christians know that the colored people will receive equal rights eventually, but it is possible that you are in too great a religious hurry. It has taken Christianity almost two thousand years to accomplish what it has. The teachings of Christ take time to come to earth." Such an attitude stems from a tragic misconception of time, from the strangely irrational notion that there is something in the very flow of time that will inevitably cure all ills. Actually, time itself is neutral; it can be used either destructively or constructively. More and more I feel that the people of ill will have used time much more effectively than have the people of good will. We will have to repent in this generation not merely for the hateful words and actions of the bad people but for the appalling silence of the good people. Human progress never rolls in on wheels of inevitability; it comes through the tireless efforts of men willing to be co workers with God, and without this hard work, time itself becomes an ally of the forces of social stagnation. We must use time creatively, in the knowledge that the time is always ripe to do right. Now is the time to make real the promise of democracy and transform our pending national elegy into a creative psalm of brotherhood. Now is the time to lift our national policy from the quicksand of racial injustice to the solid rock of human dignity.

You speak of our activity in Birmingham as extreme. At first I was rather disappointed that fellow clergymen would see my nonviolent efforts as those of an extremist. I began thinking about the fact that I stand in the middle of two opposing forces in the Negro community. One is a force of complacency, made up in part of Negroes who, as a result of long years of oppression, are so drained of self respect and a sense of "somebodiness" that they have adjusted to segregation; and in part of a few middle-class Negroes who, because of a degree of academic and economic security and because in some ways they profit by segregation, have become insensitive to the problems of the masses. The other force is one of bitterness and hatred, and it comes perilously close to advocating violence. It is expressed in the various black nationalist groups that are springing up across the nation, the largest and best known being Elijah Muhammad's Muslim movement. Nourished by the Negro's frustration over the continued existence of racial discrimination, this movement is made up of people who have lost faith in America, who have absolutely repudiated Christianity, and who have concluded that the white man is an incorrigible "devil."

I have tried to stand between these two forces, saying that we need emulate neither the "do nothingism" of the complacent nor the hatred and despair of the black nationalist. For there is the more excellent way of love and nonviolent protest. I am grateful to God that, through the influence of the Negro church, the way of nonviolence became an integral part of our struggle. If this philosophy had not emerged, by now many streets of the South would, I am convinced, be flowing with blood. And I am further convinced that if our white brothers dismiss as "rabble rousers" and "outside agitators" those of us who employ nonviolent direct action, and if they refuse to support our nonviolent efforts, millions of Negroes will, out of frustration and despair, seek solace and security in black nationalist ideologies—a development that would inevitably lead to a frightening racial nightmare.

Oppressed people cannot remain oppressed forever. The yearning for freedom eventually manifests itself, and that is what has happened to the American Negro. Something within has reminded him of his birthright of freedom, and something without has reminded him that it can be gained. Consciously or unconsciously, he has been caught up by the Zeitgeist, and with his black brothers of Africa and his brown and yellow brothers of Asia, South America and the Caribbean, the United States Negro is moving with a sense of great urgency toward the promised land of racial justice. If one recognizes this vital urge that has engulfed the Negro community, one should readily understand why public demonstrations are taking place. The Negro has many pent up resentments and latent frustrations, and he must release them. So let him march; let him make prayer pilgrimages to the city hall; let him go on freedom rides—and try to understand why he must do so. If his repressed emotions are not released in nonviolent ways, they will seek expression through violence; this is not a threat but a fact of history. So I have not said to my people: "Get rid of your discontent." Rather, I have tried to say that this normal and healthy discontent can be channeled into the creative outlet of nonviolent direct action. And now this approach is being termed extremist. But though I was initially disappointed at being categorized as an extremist, as I continued to think about the matter I gradually gained a measure of satisfaction from the label. Was not Jesus an extremist for love: "Love your enemies, bless them that curse you, do good to them that hate you, and pray for them which despitefully use you, and persecute you." Was not Amos an extremist for justice: "Let justice roll down like waters and righteousness like an ever flowing stream." Was not Paul an extremist for the Christian gospel: "I bear in my body the marks of the Lord Jesus." Was not Martin Luther an extremist: "Here I stand; I cannot do otherwise, so help me God." And John Bunyan: "I will stay in jail to the end of my days before I make a butchery of my conscience." And Abraham Lincoln: "This nation cannot survive half slave and half free." And Thomas Jefferson: "We hold these truths to be self evident, that all men are created equal . . ." So the question is not whether we will be extremists, but what kind of extremists we will be. Will we be extremists for hate or for love? Will we be extremists for the preservation of injustice or for the extension of justice? In that dramatic scene on Calvary's hill three men were crucified. We must never forget that all three were crucified for the same crime—the crime of extremism. Two were extremists for immorality, and thus fell below their environment. The other, Jesus Christ, was an extremist for love, truth and goodness, and thereby rose above his environment. Perhaps the South, the nation and the world are in dire need of creative extremists.

I had hoped that the white moderate would see this need. Perhaps I was too optimistic; perhaps I expected too much. I suppose I should have realized that few members of the oppressor race can understand the deep groans and passionate yearnings of the oppressed race, and still fewer have the vision to see that injustice must be rooted out by strong, persistent and determined action. I am thankful, however, that some of our white brothers in the South have grasped the meaning of this social revolution and committed themselves to it. They are still all too few in quantity, but they are big in quality. Some— such as Ralph McGill, Lillian Smith, Harry Golden, James McBride Dabbs, Ann

Braden and Sarah Patton Boyle—have written about our struggle in eloquent and prophetic terms. Others have marched with us down nameless streets of the South. They have languished in filthy, roach infested jails, suffering the abuse and brutality of policemen who view them as "dirty nigger-lovers." Unlike so many of their moderate brothers and sisters, they have recognized the urgency of the moment and sensed the need for powerful "action" antidotes to combat the disease of segregation. Let me take note of my other major disappointment. I have been so greatly disappointed with the white church and its leadership. Of course, there are some notable exceptions. I am not unmindful of the fact that each of you has taken some significant stands on this issue. I commend you, Reverend Stallings, for your Christian stand on this past Sunday, in welcoming Negroes to your worship service on a nonsegregated basis. I commend the Catholic leaders of this state for integrating Spring Hill College several years ago.

But despite these notable exceptions, I must honestly reiterate that I have been disappointed with the church. I do not say this as one of those negative critics who can always find something wrong with the church. I say this as a minister of the gospel, who loves the church; who was nurtured in its bosom; who has been sustained by its spiritual blessings and who will remain true to it as long as the cord of life shall lengthen.

When I was suddenly catapulted into the leadership of the bus protest in Montgomery, Alabama, a few years ago, I felt we would be supported by the white church. I felt that the white ministers, priests and rabbis of the South would be among our strongest allies. Instead, some have been outright opponents, refusing to understand the freedom movement and misrepresenting its leaders; all too many others have been more cautious than courageous and have remained silent behind the anesthetizing security of stained glass windows.

In spite of my shattered dreams, I came to Birmingham with the hope that the white religious leadership of this community would see the justice of our cause and, with deep moral concern, would serve as the channel through which our just grievances could reach the power structure. I had hoped that each of you would understand. But again I have been disappointed.

I have heard numerous Southern religious leaders admonish their worshipers to comply with a desegregation decision because it is the law, but

I have longed to hear white ministers declare: "Follow this decree because integration is morally right and because the Negro is your brother." In the midst of blatant injustices inflicted upon the Negro, I have watched white churchmen stand on the sideline and mouth pious irrelevancies and sanctimonious trivialities. In the midst of a mighty struggle to rid our nation of racial and economic injustice, I have heard many ministers say: "Those are social issues, with which the gospel has no real concern." And I have watched many churches commit themselves to a completely other worldly religion which makes a strange, un-Biblical distinction between body and soul, between the sacred and the secular.

I have traveled the length and breadth of Alabama, Mississippi and all the other southern states. On sweltering summer days and crisp autumn mornings I have looked at the South's beautiful churches with their lofty spires pointing heavenward. I have beheld the impressive outlines of her massive religious education buildings. Over and over I have found myself asking: "What kind of people worship here? Who is their God? Where were their voices when the lips of Governor Barnett dripped with words of interposition and nullification? Where were they when Governor Wallace gave a clarion call for defiance and hatred? Where were their voices of support when bruised and weary Negro men and women decided to rise from the dark dungeons of complacency to the bright hills of creative protest?"

Yes, these questions are still in my mind. In deep disappointment I have wept over the laxity of the church. But be assured that my tears have been tears of love. There can be no deep disappointment where there is not deep love. Yes, I love the church. How could I do otherwise? I am in the rather unique position of being the son, the grandson and the great grandson of preachers. Yes, I see the church as the body of Christ. But, oh! How we have blemished and scarred that body through social neglect and through fear of being nonconformists.

There was a time when the church was very powerful—in the time when the early Christians rejoiced at being deemed worthy to suffer for what they believed. In those days the church was not merely a thermometer that recorded the ideas and principles of popular opinion; it was a thermostat that transformed the mores of society. Whenever the early Christians entered a town, the people in power became disturbed and immediately sought to convict the Christians for being "disturbers of the peace" and "outside agitators."'" But the Christians pressed on, in the conviction that they were "a colony of heaven," called to obey God rather than man. Small in number, they were big in commitment. They were too God-intoxicated to be "astronomically intimidated." By their effort and example they brought an end to such ancient evils as infanticide and gladiatorial contests. Things are different now. So often the contemporary church is a weak, ineffectual voice with an uncertain sound. So often it is an archdefender of the status quo. Far from being disturbed by the presence of the church, the power structure of the average community is consoled by the church's silent—and often even vocal—sanction of things as they are.

But the judgment of God is upon the church as never before. If today's church does not recapture the sacrificial spirit of the early church, it will lose its authenticity, forfeit the loyalty of millions, and be dismissed as an irrelevant social club with no meaning for the twentieth century. Every day I meet young people whose disappointment with the church has turned into outright disgust.

Perhaps I have once again been too optimistic. Is organized religion too inextricably bound to the status quo to save our nation and the world? Perhaps I must turn my faith to the inner spiritual church, the church within the church, as the true ekklesia and the hope of the world. But again I am thankful to God that some noble souls from the ranks of organized religion have broken loose from the paralyzing chains of conformity and joined us as active partners in the struggle for freedom. They have left their secure congregations and walked the streets of Albany, Georgia, with us. They have gone down the highways of the South on tortuous rides for freedom. Yes, they have gone to jail with us. Some have been dismissed from their churches, have lost the support of their bishops and fellow ministers. But they have acted in the faith that right defeated is stronger than evil triumphant. Their witness has been the spiritual salt that has preserved the true meaning of the gospel in these troubled times. They have carved a tunnel of hope through the dark mountain of disappointment. I hope the church as a whole will meet the challenge of this decisive hour. But even if the church does not come to the aid of justice, I have no despair about the future. I have no fear about the outcome of our struggle in Birmingham, even if our motives are at present misunderstood. We will reach the goal of freedom in Birmingham and all over the nation, because the goal of America is freedom. Abused and scorned though we may be, our destiny is tied up with America's destiny. Before the pilgrims landed at Plymouth, we were here. Before the pen of Jefferson etched the majestic words of the Declaration of Independence across the pages of history, we were here. For more than two centuries our forebears labored in this country without wages; they made cotton king; they built the homes of their masters while suffering gross injustice and shameful humiliation—and yet out of a bottomless vitality they continued to thrive and develop. If the inexpressible cruelties of slavery could not stop us, the opposition we now face will surely fail. We will win our freedom because the sacred heritage of our nation and the eternal will of God are embodied in our echoing demands. Before closing I feel impelled to mention one other point in your statement that has troubled me profoundly. You warmly commended the Birmingham police force for keeping "order" and "preventing violence." I doubt that you would have so warmly commended the police force if you had seen its dogs sinking their teeth into unarmed, nonviolent Negroes. I doubt that you would so quickly commend the policemen if you were to observe their ugly and inhumane treatment of Negroes here in the city jail; if you were to watch them push and curse old Negro women and young Negro girls; if you were to see them slap and kick old Negro men and young boys; if you were to observe them, as they did on two occasions, refuse to give us food because we wanted to sing our grace together. I cannot join you in your praise of the Birmingham police department.

It is true that the police have exercised a degree of discipline in handling the demonstrators. In this sense they have conducted themselves rather "nonviolently" in public. But for what purpose? To preserve the evil system of segregation. Over the past few years I have consistently preached that nonviolence demands that the means we use must be as pure as the ends we seek. I have tried to make clear that it is wrong to use immoral means to attain moral ends. But now I must affirm that it is just as wrong, or perhaps even more so, to use moral means to preserve immoral ends. Perhaps Mr. Connor and his policemen have been rather nonviolent in public, as was Chief Pritchett in Albany, Georgia, but they have used the moral means of nonviolence to maintain the immoral end of racial injustice. As T. S. Eliot has said: "The last temptation is the greatest treason: To do the right deed for the wrong reason."

I wish you had commended the Negro sit inners and demonstrators of Birmingham for their sublime courage, their willingness to suffer and their amazing discipline in the midst of great provocation. One day the South will recognize its real heroes. They will be the James Merediths, with the noble sense of purpose that enables them to face jeering and hostile mobs, and with the agonizing loneliness that characterizes the life of the pioneer. They will be old, oppressed, battered Negro women, symbolized in a seventy two year old woman in Montgomery, Alabama, who rose up with a sense of dignity and with her people decided not to ride segregated buses, and who responded with ungrammatical profundity to one who inquired about her weariness: "My feets is tired, but my soul is at rest." They will be the young high school and college students, the young ministers of the gospel and a host of their elders, courageously and nonviolently sitting in at lunch counters and willingly going to jail for conscience' sake. One day the South will know that when these disinherited children of God sat down at lunch counters, they were in reality standing up for what is best in the American dream and for the most sacred values in our Judaeo Christian heritage, thereby bringing our nation back to those great wells of democracy which were dug deep by the founding fathers in their formulation of the Constitution and the Declaration of Independence.

Never before have I written so long a letter. I'm afraid it is much too long to take your precious time. I can assure you that it would have been much shorter if I had been writing from a comfortable desk, but what else can one do when he is alone in a narrow jail cell, other than write long letters, think long thoughts and pray long prayers?

If I have said anything in this letter that overstates the truth and indicates an unreasonable impatience, I beg you to forgive me. If I have said anything that understates the truth and indicates my having a patience that allows me to settle for anything less than brotherhood, I beg God to forgive me.

I hope this letter finds you strong in the faith. I also hope that circumstances will soon make it possible for me to meet each of you, not as an integrationist or a civil-rights leader but as a fellow clergyman and a Christian brother. Let us all hope that the dark clouds of racial prejudice will soon pass away and the deep fog of misunderstanding will be lifted from our fear drenched communities, and in some not too distant tomorrow the radiant stars of love and brotherhood will shine over our great nation with all their scintillating beauty.

Yours for the cause of Peace and Brotherhood,

Martin Luther King Jr.